31 Days with God
FOR MOTHERS

BARBOUR
PUBLISHING

© 2008 by Barbour Publishing, Inc.

Material taken from *Daily Wisdom for Mothers* by Michelle Medlock Adams.

ISBN 978-1-60260-016-4

Published by Barbour Publishing, Inc., P.O. Box 719, Uhrichsville, Ohio 44683, www.barbourbooks.com

Our mission is to publish and distribute inspirational products offering exceptional value and biblical encouragement to the masses.

Member of the
Evangelical Christian
Publishers Association

Printed in the United States of America.

TIME FOR A BREAK

*"Come to me, all you who
are weary and burdened,
and I will give you rest."*
MATTHEW 11:28

Ahh. . .rest. Who wouldn't love a day of rest? But let's face it. Mothers don't really get a day of rest. If we rested, who would fix breakfast? Who would get the children ready for church? Who would do the laundry so your son can wear his lucky socks for the big game on Monday?

No, there's not a lot of rest in a mother's schedule. But that's not really the kind of rest this verse is talking about. The rest mentioned in this verse is the kind of rest that only Jesus can provide. Resting in Jesus means feeling secure in Him and allowing His peace to fill your soul. That kind of rest is available to all—even mothers.

So, in the midst of the hustle and bustle of your life (even if you're elbow deep in dishwater), you can rest in Him. Start by meditating on the Lord's promises and His everlasting love for you. Make a mental list of the things in your life that you are thankful for and praise God for each one. Allow His love to overwhelm you. . .and rest.

MOM TO MASTER

Lord, help me to rest in You—even when I'm overwhelmed with the "To Do's" of each day. I want more of You in my life. I love You. Amen.

If peace be in the heart, the wildest winter storm is full of solemn beauty.
C. F. RICHARDSON

WORRYWARTS

"Martha, Martha," the Lord answered, "you are worried and upset about many things, but only one thing is needed. Mary has chosen what is better, and it will not be taken away from her."
LUKE 10:41–42

Do you remember when you were pregnant? In the midst of weird food cravings, swollen ankles, and raging hormones you spent time dreaming of your baby. You wondered things like: "What will he or she look like?" "What will be his or her first words?" "Will he or she be healthy?" and "How will I ever care for a tiny little baby?"

I think every mother worries. It seems like the natural thing to do. Most first-time moms worry that they won't be equipped with the appropriate parenting skills needed to be a good mom. Then the baby comes—and with it, a whole new set of worries. As the child grows, the worries grow, too. Sometimes, the worries can become almost suffocating.

When I feel overwhelmed with the worries that accompany motherhood, I realize I've forgotten to figure God into the equation. With God, all things are possible—even raising good kids in a mixed-up world. God doesn't expect mothers to have all the answers, but He does expect us to go to Him for those answers. So, if worries are consuming your thoughts—go to God. He not only has the answers, He *is* the answer!

Mom to Master

God, I trust You with my children, and I give You my worries. Amen.

Let the ways of childish confidence and
freedom from care. . .teach you what
should be your ways with God.
HANNAH WHITALL SMITH

UNCONDITIONAL LOVE

I trust in God's unfailing love for ever and ever.
PSALM 52:8

Sometimes it's harder to walk in love than others. Can I get an "Amen!" on that? There are days when my love walk has quite a limp. On those days, I often wonder how God can still love me. Ever wondered that yourself? I'll think back over something I've said or done that was less than lovely, and my insides cringe.

This is especially true when it comes to my children. Of all the people in my life, I want to make sure I show my kids that unconditional, always-there-for-you kind of love. So when I fail to accomplish that goal, my heart hurts. But it's in those times that I sense the Father's presence in a big way. I can literally feel His love wrapping around me like a cozy sweater.

No matter how many times I fail, God still loves me. And, on those days when I know I'm definitely not in the running for "Mother of the Year," that's good to know. God loves us even more than we love our children. In fact, the Word says that we're the apple of His eye. I like that. So, the next time your love walk becomes more of a crawl, remember— God adores you.

MOM TO MASTER

Heavenly Father, thank You for loving me even when I am less than loving. Amen.

Love comforteth like sunshine after rain.
WILLIAM SHAKESPEARE

EARTH TO MOM...

Let the wise listen and add to their learning.

PROVERBS 1:5

Listening. It's almost a lost art form in today's world. Yet according to the International Listening Association, "Being listened to spells the difference between feeling accepted and feeling isolated." Wow, that's pretty strong, isn't it?

In professional circles, I am a good listener. I understand the importance of listening to my colleagues; yet, I sometimes fail to listen to my children. I find myself interrupting them, trying to get them to "get to the end of the story" while I am still young. But, that's not what I should be doing as a caring, accepting mom. The Lord convicted me about this very thing not long ago, and I've been working on my listening skills ever since.

Are you a good listener? Do you really give your kids your full attention when they are talking to you? Do you nod your head and smile, letting them know that you're truly into what they are saying? If not, you may need to ask God to help you improve your listening skills, too. If we fail to listen to them now, we'll be sorry later when they no longer choose to tell us things. So go ahead. Open up your ears and your heart and listen to your children!

Mom to Master

Lord, please help me to listen to my children the same way that You listen to me. Amen.

The first duty of love is to listen.
PAUL TILLICH

STOPPING TO PRAY

But when you pray, go into your room, close the door and pray to your Father, who is unseen.
MATTHEW 6:6

Do you have a sort of bedtime ritual with your children? Some parents read a storybook to their children every night. Other parents share a Bible story or two. Some even make up their own stories to share. Whatever your bedtime routine might be, I hope that prayer is part of it.

Saying a bedtime prayer with your children is one of the most important things you can do for them. It accomplishes several things, such as teaching your kids to pray by hearing you pray aloud, giving prayer a place of importance in their lives, making prayer a habit for them, drawing the family unit closer, and enriching their spiritual side. To put it in the words of my daughter Allyson, "Prayer rocks!"

We spend so much time just doing "stuff" with our kids—running them to soccer practice, helping with homework, playing board games—and all of that is good. But if we don't figure prayer time into the daily equation, we're just spinning our wheels. Prayer time is a precious time. Don't miss out on it even one night. It's a habit worth forming!

MOM TO MASTER

Father, help me to teach my children the importance of prayer time. Amen.

My mother was the source from which I
derived the guiding principles of my life.
JOHN WESLEY

A No Good,
Very Bad Day

*Cast all your anxiety on him
because he cares for you.*
1 PETER 5:7

Ever have one of those days? The alarm clock didn't go off. The kids were late for school. The dog threw up on the carpet. You spilled coffee down the front of your new white blouse. Ahh! It's one of those "Calgon, take me away!" days, right?

But it doesn't have to be. No matter how many challenges you face today, you can smile in the face of aggravation. How? By casting your cares upon the Lord. That's what the Lord tells us to do in His Word, yet many of us feel compelled to take all of the cares upon ourselves. After all, we're mothers. We're fixers. We're the doers of the bunch. We wear five or six fedoras at a time—we can handle anything that comes our way, right?

Wrong! But God can. When the day starts to go south, cast your cares on Him. He *wants* you to! As mothers, we can handle a lot, but it's true what they say—Father really does know best. So, give it to God. C'mon, you know you want to. . . .

MOM TO MASTER

Lord, help me to turn to You when my troubles seem too big to face alone and even when they don't. Help me to trust You with all of my cares. Amen.

Thou art coming to a King
Large petitions with thee bring;
For His grace and power are such
None can ever ask too much.
JOHN NEWTON

WONDERFUL
WEAKNESSES

*But he said to me, "My grace is sufficient for you, for my
power is made perfect in weakness." Therefore I will
boast all the more gladly about my weaknesses, so that
Christ's power may rest on me.*
2 CORINTHIANS 12:9

Nobody likes to admit weaknesses but, hey, we've all got them. The good news is this—God can work with weakness. In fact, His Word tells us that His power is made perfect in our weakness. Pretty cool, eh? So, why is it so difficult to admit we have weaknesses?

I'll be honest. I hate to admit that I have weaknesses—especially with my children. I like to appear perfect and "superhero-like." I want Abby and Allyson to think they've got the coolest mom in the world—a mom who loves God, loves them, and can still skateboard with the best of them. But over the past few years, I am pretty sure my daughters have figured out that Mom has got some weaknesses—definitely! The cat is out of the bag, so to speak.

And I'm okay with that. If we let our children see our shortcomings, they'll feel better about their own weaknesses. So quit trying to disguise your weaknesses or make excuses for them. Just admit you've got them and let God's power be made perfect in them.

MOM TO MASTER

Father, thank You for working through my weaknesses. Amen.

As a countenance is made beautiful by the soul's shining through it, so the world is beautiful by the shining through it of God.
FRIEDRICH HEINRICH JACOBI

THANKSGIVING ISN'T JUST FOR NOVEMBER

Consider it pure joy, my brothers,
whenever you face trials of many kinds.
JAMES 1:2

I recently visited a Web site that made me feel a bit guilty for all the times that I've complained about everyday stuff. Its headline said:

THINGS TO BE THANKFUL FOR

- The taxes I pay—because it means that I'm employed.
- The clothes that fit snugly—because it means I have enough to eat.
- The mounds of laundry—because it means I have clothes to wear.

Okay, be honest. Have you ever been thankful for taxes, extra weight, or loads of laundry? Me neither. But it is an interesting concept. It does make you think, doesn't it? We should be looking for reasons to be thankful—even in the stuff that would not ordinarily fill our hearts with gratitude.

And, we should impart that same attitude into our kids. They'll be much happier children if they'll take that stance in life. So when your daughter doesn't get invited to "the big party," she can be thankful that she has a mom who will take her to the movies instead. Or when your son doesn't make the football team, he can be thankful that he has more free time to practice his guitar. It's really about looking for that silver lining in every gray cloud. Find that silver lining today.

MOM TO MASTER

Lord, I praise You for the good and not-so-good things in my life. Amen.

Throughout life we hardly realize that we receive a great deal more than we give. It is only with gratitude that life becomes rich.

DIETRICH BONHOEFFER

MOVIE-STAR DREAMS

*I can do everything through him
who gives me strength.*
PHILIPPIANS 4:13

W hat do you want to be when you grow up?" I asked my daughter, Ally, when she was only four.

She thought for a moment and then she answered matter-of-factly, "A movie star."

"Great," I responded. "Then you can pay for Mommy's and Daddy's retirement condo in Florida."

Children know how to dream big. Do you know why? Because no one has told them yet that they can't dream big. I love that about kids. They don't have that inner voice going that says, "You can't be a movie star. You're not good enough. You're not pretty enough. You'll never be able to accomplish your dream." No, they believe they can do anything. And you know what? They're right! God's Word says that we can do all things through Christ who gives us strength. *All* means *all*, right?

That's why Jesus said we should have childlike faith. We should be able to believe *big* when it comes to the dreams and ambitions that God has placed within us. God wouldn't have placed them there if He weren't going to help us achieve them. So learn from your kids. Get back that childlike faith and start believing.

MOM TO MASTER

Lord, help me to believe You like my children believe You. Help me to dream big like they do. Amen.

Far away, there in the sunshine,
are my highest aspirations. . . . I can
look up and see their beauty, believe in
them, and try to follow where they lead.
LOUISA MAY ALCOTT

Your B.F.F.
(Best Friend Forever)

Trust in God. Lean on your God!
Isaiah 50:10 MSG

Do you remember that song "Lean on Me" by Al Green? I think Club Nouveau remade it back in the '80s. I love the words to that song. I've always thought of it as rather inspirational in nature. Do you remember the words? "Lean on me. When you're not strong. I'll be your friend. I'll help you carry on." (You're singing along right now, aren't you?)

If there's anything moms need, it's someone to lean on from time to time. Can I get an amen, sister? When the dishwasher is broken, the car is in the shop, the kids are sick, and your bank account is empty and payday is a week away. . .we all need somebody to lean on.

I'm so thankful that we have God to lean on during difficult times. Even if our family or friends don't understand our feelings and even if there's no one else to lean on, we've always got God. He promises in His Word to never leave us nor forsake us. We can lean on Him, and He's happy to let us. So, if you're having a lousy day, a lousy week, or even a lousy year, God understands and He loves you. Go ahead—lean on Him. He will be your Friend.

MOM TO MASTER

Thank You, Lord, that I can lean on You. Thanks
for always being there for me. Amen.

When you have accomplished your daily
tasks, go to sleep in peace. God is awake.
VICTOR HUGO

Under the Influence

Dear children, do not let anyone lead you astray.
1 John 3:7

Do you ever worry about the friends that your children are making? I do. I often wonder, *Will they be good influences on my children? Will they hurt my children? Do they know Jesus as their Lord and Savior? Will they be lifelong, trustworthy friends?*

While I don't know the answers to all of these questions, I do know one thing—Jesus will be their lifelong friend. They will always be able to count on Him. He will come through for them time and time again. He will stand by them no matter what. How do I know these things? Because He's been there for me when nobody else was.

I discovered early in life that friends sometimes let you down—even your best friends—because they're human. If you put your hope in friends, disappointment and hurt are inevitable. But God is a sure thing.

I realize that I can't pick my children's friends, and I know that I can't protect them from the hurt that comes from broken friendships and disloyalty. But there are two things I *can* do—I can teach them about Jesus, and I can pray that the Lord sends them godly friends. You can do the same for your kids. You can start today.

Mom to Master

*Lord, please send my children good friends. I'm
thankful that You're their best friend and mine.
Amen.*

Beneath God's watchful eye
His saints securely dwell;
That hand which bears all nature up
Shall guard His children well.
WILLIAM COWPER

IT'S YOUR TURN!

And the people, that is, the men of Israel,
encouraged themselves.
JUDGES 20:22 NKJV

Do you ever encourage yourself in the Lord? As moms, we encourage everybody else—our husbands, our children, our friends, our extended family, and our neighbors. But we rarely take time to encourage ourselves. Instead, we're overly critical of ourselves. We allow the devil to beat us up, telling us how awful we are. If we'll listen long enough, the devil will convince us that we're unworthy to be servants of God. He'll tell us that we're horrible parents and wives. He'll tell us that we're failures in life. The devil will serve us condemnation with a side of guilt as often as we'll let him. So tell him, *"No more!"*

We have to stop allowing the devil to deceive us. Don't dwell on his lies; meditate on God's Word. The Bible says that you are fully able to fulfill your destiny. It says that no weapon formed against you is going to prosper. It says that you can do everything through God's strength. Stop focusing on what you can't do and start focusing on what you can do. Quit looking at how far you've got to go, and start looking at how far you've already come. Encourage yourself in the Lord today! It's your turn.

Mom to Master

Thank You, Lord, for giving me the ability to fulfill my destiny. Help me to stay encouraged. Amen.

You are special. God made you. His undeserved love makes you somebody!

ALMA KERN

EXTRAORDINARY REQUIREMENTS

*"And I tell you that you are Peter, and on
this rock I will build my church, and the
gates of Hades will not overcome it."*
MATTHEW 16:18

Did you know that God loves to use ordinary people to do extraordinary things?

Look at Peter. He was just a fisherman, but God called him "the rock upon which I will build my church."

What about Mary? She was an unmarried teenager, but God chose her to give birth to Jesus.

How about David? He was the little guy in the family. When his brothers went to war, he had to stay at home and watch over the sheep. Still, God called him to defeat the giant. Amazing, isn't it?

If you're feeling like you're not cut out for this motherhood job, cheer up! God is using you to do extraordinary things for His kingdom, too. He wouldn't have entrusted you with your precious children if He didn't believe you could handle it. Of course, it's difficult some days. But, hey, God is a big God—bigger than all of our doubts, transgressions, and faults. You don't have to be perfect. You just have to be available. Open your heart and let God restore your hope today. He has more extraordinary things in store for you!

MOM TO MASTER

Lord, do the extraordinary in me and through me today. Amen.

The shocking message of the Bible
continues to be that God has chosen
the least suspecting of all vessels to
do his greatest work. What you are at
this particular moment in your life is
irrelevant—your nationality, your education,
your personality. . . . What counts most is
what and *who* you are willing to become.
TIM HANSEL

GETTING RID OF THE GROUCHIES

[Love] doesn't fly off the handle.
1 CORINTHIANS 13:5 MSG

How is your attitude today? Feeling kind of grouchy? There are mornings that I open my eyes and just feel grouchy. It's as if the devil was waiting for me to get up so he could use my mouth to say ugly things. Ever been there? On those days, I have to force myself to walk in love. Let's face it. If you haven't been sleeping enough, or if you're under quite a bit of stress, or if you're feeling ill, it's easier to be a grouch.

But moms aren't supposed to be grouches! Haven't you ever seen *Leave It to Beaver* on TV Land? Mrs. Cleaver is always joyful. And how about that Carol Brady on *The Brady Bunch*? She is so sweet that it's sickening!

In reality, no mom can be perfect all the time. We all lose our tempers. We all complain. We all act ugly. We all get grouchy. But God knew that when He created us. He knew our flesh would win out once in a while. That's why He sent Jesus to save us from our sins, so we can repent for our grouchy attitudes and move forward in love. So get those grouchies off and let love control you today.

MOM TO MASTER

Lord, flood me with Your love. Amen.

For every minute you are angry,
you lose sixty seconds of happiness.
AUTHOR UNKNOWN

WISE UP!

Timely advice is lovely, like golden
apples in a silver basket.
PROVERBS 25:11 NLT

It's funny—as young children we thought our moms knew everything. As teens, we thought they knew nothing. As adults, we realize we were right in the first place—they do know everything. Moms are full of wisdom; however, when I became a mom I didn't feel so wise. In fact, I didn't know the first thing about being a mother. As I've matured, I've learned a little about being a mom—mostly from my mom. Her advice is priceless.

We can learn much from the godly women in our lives. Maybe your mom hasn't been there for you but God has placed other women in your life—an aunt, a grandmother, a close family friend, or your pastor's wife. Cherish their words of wisdom. God has placed them in your life for a purpose.

Just think, some day your children will look to you for wisdom—it's true! The Word says that they will rise up and call you blessed. So make sure you have some wisdom to share. Treasure the advice that's been given to you and, more importantly, meditate on the Word of God. There's much wisdom waiting for you!

Mom to Master

Heavenly Father, thank You for those special women in my life. Help me to honor them and You. Amen.

Knowledge is horizontal.
Wisdom is vertical—
it comes down from above.
Billy Graham

SUPERNATURAL ACCOUNTABILITY

My brothers, can a fig tree bear olives, or a grapevine bear figs? Neither can a salt spring produce fresh water.
JAMES 3:12

We know from the Word of God that the tongue is hard to tame. Of course, I didn't need the Bible to tell me that fact. I am well aware that my mouth is hard to control. Maybe you have that same challenge. That's why this scripture really brings conviction to me. If you're praising the Lord in church and hollering at your children on the way home, this scripture probably hits home with you, too.

We need to continually ask the Lord to put a watch on our mouths. We need to ask for His help so that we might be good examples for our children. If they see us praising God one minute and hollering at them the next, they will be confused and disillusioned with the things of God.

James 3:9 says, "With the tongue we praise our Lord and Father, and with it we curse men, who have been made in God's likeness." We must be careful of our words because not only are our children listening, God is also listening. And we'll be held accountable for our words—all of them.

MOM TO MASTER

Lord, please put a watch on my mouth that I might only speak good things. Help me to be a good example for my children. I love You. Amen.

Live so that your [children] will have a role model within arm's reach at all times.

VICKIE PHELPS

TAXI TIME-OUT

Cast your cares on the LORD and he will sustain you;
he will never let the righteous fall.
PSALM 55:22

There are days when I'm sure the side of my SUV must say "Taxi." We run to gymnastics. We race to cheerleading practice. We rush to art class. We hurry to Girl Scouts. We eat fast food on the way to computer class.

I want to stand up and say, "Stop the world from spinning! I want to get off!"

There is such pressure these days to make sure our children are in every extracurricular activity that sometimes I wonder if it's all too much. Have you been wondering the same thing?

We're moms. It's only natural that we desire to give our children the best. So it's no wonder we sign them up for all of these wonderful extracurricular opportunities. But be careful. Make sure you're not pushing and nudging your children right into burnout. We don't want our kids to be so overwhelmed with activities that they have no time to be kids. They only get one childhood. Ask God to help you enhance their growing up years without overwhelming them with "stuff." Even good stuff, if there's too much of it, can be bad.

MOM TO MASTER

Lord, help me not to pressure my children with too much "stuff," but help me to encourage the gifts that You have put inside them. Amen.

Fill up the crevices of time with the things that matter most.
AMY CARMICHAEL

GIMME-VILLE

"But seek first his kingdom and his righteousness,
and all these things will be given to you as well."
MATTHEW 6:33

Do your kids ever get the "Gimme Syndrome"? You know, the "Gimme this" and "Gimme that" phase. We've lived through a few of those in our house. Of course, there are the "terrible twos" when everything is "Mine!" And, then the tweens seem to bring out the "Gimmes" in a more expensive way. Instead of "Gimme that sucker," it's "Gimme that Go-Kart." (I wonder if the teen years will give birth to the "Gimme that Corvette!")

No matter the season, the "Gimme Syndrome" is bad. You see, "Gimmes" always lead to more "Gimmes." The Bible might say it like this: "Gimmes beget gimmes." Once you fulfill the first "Gimme requests," there are always more to follow. It's continual!

But if we seek God first, all of our wants and "Gimmes" will be fulfilled. We need to keep our "Gimmes" under control and focus our energies on seeking God. If we breed little "Gimme" kids, they'll carry that mentality over into their relationship with God. Their prayers will be filled with, "Hi God. Gimme this and Gimme that. Amen." Ask God to get the "Gimmes" out of your household today. That's one request He'll be happy to fulfill!

Mom to Master

Lord, I pray that You remove the "Gimme" attitude from my household. Amen.

Thou hast given so much to me,
Give one thing more—a grateful heart;
Not thankful when it pleaseth me,
As if Thy blessings had spare days,
But such a heart whose pulse
may be Thy praise.
George Herbert

By the Grace of God

*. . .because of the surpassing grace God has given you.
Thanks be to God for his indescribable gift!*
2 Corinthians 9:14–15

Grace. We say grace. We name baby girls Grace. But do we really understand how wonderful God's grace is in our lives? I wouldn't want to live one second without it operating in my life. Grace is defined as "God's unmerited favor." In other words, we didn't earn it. We certainly didn't deserve it, but God gave us His grace anyway. How great is that? And where you find grace, you almost always find mercy alongside it. Whew! That's good news, isn't it?

People who lived under the Law didn't have the luxury of grace. When they broke even the smallest rule, they were in a lot of trouble. I'm so thankful for God's grace, because I mess up on a regular basis. But when I do mess up, I can run to Him. I don't have to hide, because when I repent, He gives me grace. He says, "That's okay, you'll do better next time."

In the same manner that God shows us grace, we should show our children grace. They aren't perfect, either. They are going to mess up once in awhile. But if we show them grace, they'll run to us when they get into trouble. They won't hide from us.

MOM TO MASTER

Father, I praise You for the gift of grace. Amen.

Your worst days are never so bad that you are beyond the reach of God's grace. And your best days are never so good that you are beyond the need of God's grace.

JERRY BRIDGES

YOU WANT *ME*?

*Gideon said to him, "Me, my master?
How and with what could I ever save Israel?
Look at me. My clan's the weakest in Manasseh
and I'm the runt of the litter."*
JUDGES 6:15 MSG

Do you ever feel incapable of being a good mother? Are there days when you think, "God, are You sure I can do this?" If you ever feel inadequate, you're not alone. Women all over the world struggle with those same feelings of insecurity, self-doubt, and hopelessness. Even though you feel less than able to do all of the things on your plate, God sees you as more than able to do everything He has called you to do.

Even great leaders in the Bible felt inadequate at times. Remember what Moses said when God called him to tell Pharaoh to let the Israelites go? Moses said that he couldn't possibly do it. He told God that He had the wrong guy before finally agreeing to do it. And what about Gideon? When God called him to lead His people against Midian, he said, "I'm the weakest in Manasseh—the runt of the litter." Still, God addressed him as "You mighty man of valor." See, God didn't see Gideon as a weak worm of the dust. He saw Gideon as a mighty man of valor. God sees you as mighty and strong and capable, too! Ask God to help you see yourself as He sees you.

MOM TO MASTER

Lord, help me to see myself as You see me. I love You. Amen.

The same God who guides the stars in
their courses, who directs the earth in its
orbit, who feeds the burning furnace of
the sun and keeps the stars perpetually
burning with their fires—the same God has
promised to supply thy strength.
CHARLES SPURGEON

KNOWING GOD

*My people are ruined because they
don't know what's right or true.*
HOSEA 4:6 MSG

As moms, it's our awesome responsibility to tell our children about the things of God—that's what this verse communicates to me. If we don't tell them about salvation, they'll never know that Jesus died on the cross to save them from sin. If we don't tell them about His unconditional love, they won't run to Him in times of trouble. If we don't tell them about healing, they'll never know that God can heal their sicknesses. They need to know these important truths so that they won't perish for lack of knowledge.

Teaching our children God's Word and His ways are the two most important things we can give our kids, because if they have that knowledge, they have it all! As moms, we can't always be there for our children. But if we've equipped them with the Word of God, they will be all right without us.

It's like John Cougar Mellencamp says in one of his '80s tunes, "You've got to stand for something, or you're gonna fall for anything." If our children stand on the Word of God, they won't be easily fooled or swayed. So take the time to teach your children the Word. It's the most important investment you'll ever make.

MOM TO MASTER

Heavenly Father, help my children to love Your Word and carry it with them always. Amen.

Children are the living messages we send to a time we will not see.
JOHN W. WHITEHEAD

The Discipline of God

The rod of correction imparts wisdom,
but a child left to himself disgraces his mother.
Proverbs 29:15

No matter where you stand on the spanking issue, this verse holds good meaning. You see, it's not so much about the spanking, it's about the wisdom that we impart when we discipline our children.

There are lots of differing opinions about how to discipline our children. Some experts say we should spank them with our hands. Others say we should spank, but only with a paddle. Still others say we should never spank, only punish by other means. It seems there is a new theory every year. So what is the answer?

God is the only true answer. You must seek His face and ask His direction. He will teach you how to discipline your kids. He loves them even more than you do. He won't lead you astray. Just trust Him. Don't get caught up asking lots of people how you should discipline your kids. If you ask a hundred people, you'll get a hundred different perspectives. They don't know any more than you do. Go to the Source. He will impart wisdom to you so that you can impart wisdom to your children. You see, discipline and wisdom go hand in hand.

Mom to Master

Lord, teach me the best way to discipline my children. Amen.

Some are kissing mothers and
some are scolding mothers,
but it is love just the same—and
most mothers kiss and scold together.
PEARL S. BUCK

DON'T PUSH
MY BUTTONS!

I will praise you as long as I live.
PSALM 63:4

Have you ever watched a college cheerleading squad? Their motions are perfectly timed, in sync, on beat, and very sharp. If one member is behind a half a count, you'll be able to tell. Even minor flaws and mistakes are greatly magnified when the rest of the team is so good.

Do you ever feel like that cheerleader who is a half step behind the entire routine? I do. Sometimes it seems that all of the moms I know have it all together, and I'm kicking with the wrong leg. The devil loves to point out our shortcomings and whisper things like, "Hey, you are the worst mother ever. If you were a better mom, your children would be doing better in school."

See, the devil knows what buttons to push in order to make you feel the very worst—but don't let him have access to your buttons. When you start to compare yourself with another mother, stop yourself. Right then, begin thanking God for giving you the wisdom and strength to be the best mom you can be. When you respond to the devil's button-pushing with praise for the Father, you will send the devil packing.

MOM TO MASTER

Father, help me to be the best mom that I can be. Help me to stop comparing myself with others. I praise You. Amen.

What a relief to simply let go of my need to do everything perfectly—and instead just do everything for You! You know I'll always make mistakes; You know that sometimes my best efforts will look like failures to everybody else. Thank You that I can simply relax and trust You to work everything out according to Your plan.

DARLENE SALA

TRUE HAPPINESS

"Give, and it will be given to you: good measure pressed down, shaken together and running over. . . ."
LUKE 6:38 NKJV

Did you know that God wants you to be happy? He desires for you to live life to its fullest. It doesn't matter that you might be elbow deep in diapers or carpools right now—you can still enjoy life!

One of the main ways you can guarantee joy in your life is by living to give. You see, true happiness comes when we give of ourselves to others—our spouses, our children, our extended family, our church, our community, and our friends. As moms, we're sort of trained to be givers. We give up our careers, many times, to become full-time moms. We give up a full night's sleep to feed our babies. We give up sports cars for minivans and SUVs to accommodate our families. In fact, we'd give our lives for our children.

But sometimes our attitudes are less than joyful in all of our giving, right? Well, rejoice today. God promises to multiply back to you everything that you give. When you step out in faith, you open a door for God to move on your behalf. It's the simple principle of sowing and reaping. And as mothers, we are super sowers. So get ready for a super huge harvest!

Mom to Master

Lord, help me to live to give with the right attitude. I thank You. Amen.

Those who bring sunshine into the lives of others cannot keep it from themselves.
JAMES M. BARRIE

LETTING GO

*"I'll give him and his descendants the land he walked on
because he was all for following GOD, heart and soul."*
DEUTERONOMY 1:36 MSG

Have you ever heard the expression, "Let go and let God"? It's easier said than done. We sing songs in church about giving our all to God, such as "All to Jesus, I surrender," when all the while, we're holding something back. I'm guilty, too. So many times I have gone before God and asked Him to take over every part of my life, and then later the Holy Spirit will point out an area of my heart that I didn't give to God.

It's silly, isn't it? I don't know why we'd ever want to hold out on God. He doesn't want us to give our all so that He can make us miserable. He wants us to give our all so that He can bless us beyond our wildest dreams. God isn't some big ogre in the sky, just waiting for us to give our all to Him so that He can control us like puppets. He simply wants us to give our all so that we can walk in the plan that He has for us. So if you're struggling with giving your all today, ask God to help you. Go ahead—let go and let God. He will give you much more in return.

Mom to Master

Lord, I give my all to You today. Help me to leave my life in Your hands. Amen.

I wish for you the joy of holding life with an open hand. Just let go of all the stuff you've had to worry about and hang on to and protect. . . . It isn't what you have that determines your strength now or in the future. It is what you are willing to let go of that is the ultimate test.

BOB BENSON

ROCK. . .AND REST

He will not allow your foot to be moved;
He who keeps you will not slumber.
PSALM 121:3 NKJV

I think the world needs more rocking chairs. We were at Cracker Barrel not long ago and had to wait for a table, so we all went outside and plopped down in our own rocking chairs. I hadn't sat in a rocking chair since my girls were babies.

With each swaying movement, I was taken back to a precious memory of holding baby Abby and baby Ally in my arms. Now that they are older, they don't sit on my lap very often. They are far "too cool" for that. Sometimes, I long for those rocking chair days. Rocking chairs force you to slow down and enjoy the moment. It's almost impossible to be stressed out while rocking. Sitting in a rocking chair is like cozying up to a close, old friend. There's something very comforting and comfortable about spending time in a rocking chair.

You know, even if you don't have a rocking chair at your house, you can spend some quality rocking time in God's rocker. When I pray to the Father, I always picture Him sitting in a big, wooden rocking chair and beckoning me to sit on His lap. If you need to de-stress today, crawl into your heavenly Father's lap and rock awhile.

MOM TO MASTER

Lord, I need to spend some quality time just rocking with You today. Thanks for loving me. Amen.

Jesus knows we must come apart
and rest awhile, or else we may
just plain come apart.
VANCE HAVNER

Just What You Need

*"Your Father knows exactly what you
need even before you ask him!"*
Matthew 6:8 nlt

Have you ever been so distraught that you didn't even know what to pray? I think we've all been there at some point in our lives. After my father had his first stroke and they didn't know if he would live through the night, I became numb. It was touch and go for several days, and all I did was drive to and from the hospital. On those forty-minute drives, I would try to pray, but all I could do was say the name of Jesus. Thankfully, that was enough.

In Matthew 6:8, the Word tells us that God knows what we need even before we ask Him. That's good to know, isn't it? Even when we can't pray what we want to pray, God knows our hearts. He knows what we need. If we simply call on the name of Jesus, He is right there beside us.

No matter how desperate you are today, no matter how hopeless you feel, no matter how far from God you think you are. . .God loves you. He wants to help you. He wants to help your children. He wants to bring you through this difficult time. Call on Him today.

Mom to Master

Thank You, Lord, for knowing me so well and hearing my heart. Amen.

What seem our worst prayers may really be, in God's eyes, our best. Those, I mean, which are least supported by devotional feeling. For these may come from a deeper level than feeling. God sometimes seems to speak to us most intimately when He catches us, as it were, off our guard.

C. S. Lewis

PARROT-HOOD

"It would be better for him if a millstone were hung around his neck, and he were thrown into the sea, than that he should offend one of these little ones."
LUKE 17:2 NKJV

How is your witness? Do you know that everywhere we go, we are witnessing? We are witnessing all the time—either glorifying God or portraying a poor reflection of Him. And here's the kicker: Our children are taking it all in. They are like little sponges, absorbing everything we do and say, all the time. Wow! Have you ever thought about that reality? Our kids may be basing their view of Christianity on how we behave. Oh my!

I first realized that fact when my daughter Abby was just a toddler. She was a miniature parrot. She repeated absolutely everything I said—good or bad. Once I was on the phone with my mother, and I said that someone had acted like a horse's behind. Later that night when Allyson drooled on one of Abby's favorite dolls, Abby said, "You are a horse's behind!" While it was funny, it was sad, too. I knew exactly where she had heard the expression—from me!

So like the song says, "Be careful, little mouth, what you say," and go forth and give a good witness. You have an attentive audience nearby.

MOM TO MASTER

Lord, help me to be a good reflection of you all the time. Help me to point my children toward you. Amen.

Most of the people who will walk
after me will be children, so make
the beat keep time with short steps.
HANS CHRISTIAN ANDERSEN

REAL GROWTH

But Jesus said, "Let the little children come to Me,
and do not forbid them; for of such is the
kingdom of heaven."
MATTHEW 19:14 NKJV

Parents today are quite proactive. They have their unborn babies on waiting lists for the top preschools in the area. They have college funds established before their children have ever spoken their first words. Parents today are really thinking and planning ahead. That's a good thing; however, many parents are neglecting the most important part of their children's lives—their salvation.

While it's wonderful to put so much thought into the proper preschool for our little ones, it's much more important to make sure we're attending a church that will nurture and encourage our children's spiritual development. If you're in a church that doesn't have a strong children's ministry, it may be time to seek God for a new place of worship.

Ask the Lord to help you find the best church for your children's sake. If you're attending a church that simply entertains and baby-sits the kids, then start looking for another church. Let's face it, being a good dodgeball player isn't going to help our children when they are facing peer pressure. Let's be proactive about our children's spiritual lives. There's nothing more important.

MOM TO MASTER

Lord, please direct me to a church that will best minister to my children. Amen.

There are only two lasting bequests
we can hope to give our children.
One is roots; the other, wings.
HODDING CARTER

MOMENTARY
MEDITATION

But from everlasting to everlasting the
LORD's love is with those who fear him.
PSALM 103:17

Life is just so busy! There are some days when I can't see past the end of my nose. Deadlines, overflowing laundry baskets, soccer practice, grocery shopping. . . Tomorrow seems an eternity away, and I can't even wrap my mind around the concept of eternity. So when I read a verse that says God's love is with us from everlasting to everlasting, I don't always get it.

Lately when having my Bible study time, I've been asking God to turn off the to-do list part of my brain so that I can really hear God's voice through His Word. And you know what? It works! Suddenly, His Word leaps off the page, and all at once, I get it!

Psalm 103:17 has become one of my very favorite verses. To think that someone—especially the Creator of the universe—could love me forever and ever is so great! What a wonderful promise!

As moms we don't have a lot of time to meditate on God's Word, so we have to make the most of those moments with the Master. Ask God to help you really focus as you read the Bible. Ask Him to show you what He has especially for you on that day. It's exciting!

MOM TO MASTER

Lord, help me to meditate more on Your Word.
Amen.

In the noise and clatter of my kitchen. . .
I possess God in as great tranquillity
as if I were on my knees.
BROTHER LAWRENCE

Spiritual Fruitcake

*But the fruit of the Spirit is love, joy, peace,
patience, kindness, goodness, faithfulness,
gentleness and self-control.*
Galatians 5:22–23

Did you receive a fruit basket last Christmas? How about a fruitcake? (If not, I'll send you one of the fruitcakes that I received—yuck! I am not a fan of fruitcake.) But maybe you like fruitcake or enjoy giving fruit baskets to your friends and family members during certain times of the year.

Let me tell you what's even better than giving a fruit basket or a fruitcake—giving the fruit of the Spirit. It's one of the best ways we can ever give to or bless those around us. We don't have to just give during the holidays—we can radiate those qualities year round!

Our children need to see us walking in these qualities. They need to feel that love, joy, peace, patience, kindness, goodness, faithfulness, gentleness, and self-control operating in our homes. Sure, we're going to miss it once in a while, but as long as we're growing in those things, that's all that counts. God isn't keeping score on how many times we lose self-control; rather, He is celebrating with us as we grow in every fruit. So, go on. Give good fruit today!

MOM TO MASTER

Thank You, God, for the fruit of the Spirit. Help me to grow in each fruit so that I'll become more like You. Amen.

Joy is love exalted, peace is love in repose; long-suffering is love enduring; gentleness is love in society; goodness is love in action; faith is love on the battlefield; meekness is love in school; and temperance is love in training.
DWIGHT L. MOODY

31 Days with God
for Mothers
ISBN 978-1-60260-016-4

31 Days with God
for Grads
ISBN 978-1-60260-017-1

31 Days with God
for Fathers
ISBN 978-1-60260-018-8

ONLY 99 CENTS EACH!

AVAILABLE WHEREVER CHRISTIAN BOOKS ARE SOLD.